WOMEN IN
Literature

BY WENDY HINOTE LANIER

CONTENT CONSULTANT
Sarah Ruffing Robbins, PhD
Professor of Literature
Texas Christian University

Core Library

An Imprint of Abdo Publishing
abdopublishing.com

Cover image: J. K. Rowling attended the opening night
of the play *Harry Potter and the Cursed Child*.

abdopublishing.com

Published by Abdo Publishing, a division of ABDO, PO Box 398166, Minneapolis, Minnesota 55439. Copyright © 2019 by Abdo Consulting Group, Inc. International copyrights reserved in all countries. No part of this book may be reproduced in any form without written permission from the publisher. Core Library™ is a trademark and logo of Abdo Publishing.

Printed in the United States of America, North Mankato, Minnesota
032018
092018

THIS BOOK CONTAINS
RECYCLED MATERIALS

Cover Photo: Joel Ryan/Invision/AP Images
Interior Photos: Joel Ryan/Invision/AP Images, 1; Vianney Le Caer/Invision/AP Images, 4–5; Phelan M. Ebenhack/AP Images, 7; Yui Mok/Press Association/PA Wire URN:31179639/AP Images, 8; Warner Bros./Photofest, 10; Popperfoto/Getty Images, 12–13; Universal Studios/Photofest, 14; Red Line Editorial, 17; Joseph Lederer/Columbia Pictures/Photofest, 18, 43; Hulton Archive/Hulton Archive/Getty Images, 20–21; Larry Morris/The Washington Post/Getty Images, 25; AP images, 26–27; Shutterstock Images, 31 (top), 31 (bottom); Arsen Luben/Shutterstock Images, 31 (middle top); Serhiy Smirnov/Shutterstock Images, 31 (middle bottom); Eric Charbonneau/Invision/AP Images, 32; Astrid Riecken/The Washington Post/Getty Images, 34–35, 45; Vern Fisher/Monterey Herald/AP Images, 37; Johnny Louis/JL/Sipa USA/Newscom, 38

Editor: Julie Dick
Imprint Designer: Maggie Villaume
Series Design Direction: Claire Vanden Branden

Library of Congress Control Number: 2017962809

Publisher's Cataloging-in-Publication Data

Names: Lanier, Wendy Hinote, author.
Title: Women in literature / by Wendy Hinote Lanier.
Description: Minneapolis, Minnesota : Abdo Publishing, 2019. | Series: Women in the arts | Includes online resources and index.
Identifiers: ISBN 9781532114762 (lib.bdg.) | ISBN 9781532154591 (ebook)
Subjects: LCSH: Women authors--Juvenile literature. | Women publishers--Juvenile literature. | Literature--Women authors--Juvenile literature. | Professions--Juvenile literature.
Classification: DDC 820.992--dc23

CONTENTS

The Wizardly World of J. K. Rowling

In 1990, Joanne Rowling was riding a train into London, England. The train was delayed, leaving Rowling plenty of time to think. As she waited, Rowling came up with an idea. The idea was about a young wizard. He was a student at Hogwarts School of Witchcraft and Wizardry.

HARRY'S DEBUT

During the next few years Rowling married, had a daughter, and divorced. She became

J. K. Rowling is one of the best-known authors in the world.

a single mom trying desperately to pay her bills. But she was also a writer. She continued to make notes, write, and map out a total of seven Harry Potter books.

By the late 1990s, Rowling had finished the first Harry Potter book. It was rejected by numerous publishers. But in 1997, *Harry Potter and the Philosopher's Stone* was published in England. The publisher thought young boys would not want to read a book by a woman. They asked Rowling to shorten her name to hide her gender.

A girl tests a wand at the Wizarding World of Harry Potter in Orlando, Florida.

Joanne Rowling became J. K. Rowling. The K is for Kathleen. It was Rowling's grandmother's name.

The next year Rowling's book was published in the United States. The title was changed to *Harry Potter and the Sorcerer's Stone.* Harry and his friends were a smashing success in both England and the

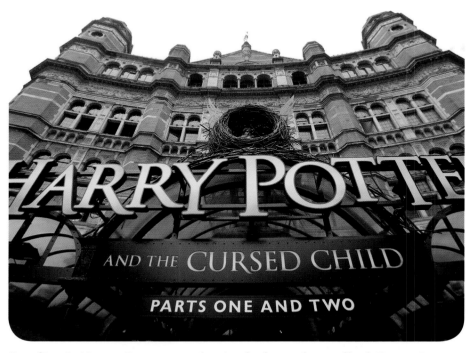

Rowling's Harry Potter stories include a play called *Harry Potter and the Cursed Child*.

United States. Two more books quickly followed. In 2001 the first book became a movie. By 2011, the Harry Potter series included seven books and eight movies. The public had waited eagerly for each new title. Sometimes they stood in long lines or waited overnight to buy the newest book. The books have sold more than 450 million copies.

AFTER HARRY POTTER

Although the Harry Potter series is finished, Rowling has written other books. Some are about Harry Potter's world. But in 2012, Rowling published her first book for adults. It is called *The Casual Vacancy.* The book has been translated into 44 languages and adapted for British television.

In 2013, Rowling began writing crime novels under a pen name, Robert Galbraith. The novels feature a private detective who is a war veteran. The first novel received mixed reviews. Some people liked it, but others did not. At first no one knew Rowling

Careers in Writing

Not all writers write the same kinds of things. People who write stories for adults are called novelists. Writers who write poetry are poets. A playwright writes plays for the stage. A screenwriter writes scripts for movies. People who write for children are children's authors. There are also many types of specialty writing. But all writers have one thing in common. They all want to communicate through their writing.

Rowling wrote the screenplay for *Fantastic Beasts and Where to Find Them*, the story of wizard Newt Scamander and his magical creatures.

was the author. When her identity as the author was revealed, the books became an instant hit. Three books were published by 2017, with another book in progress. The series was adapted into a crime drama in 2017.

ROWLING TODAY

Rowling continues to write for children and adults. In 2016, she wrote a story that was adapted for the stage. The play won several awards. She also wrote the screenplay for the film *Fantastic Beasts and Where to Find Them*. The movie is a prequel to the Harry Potter series. The story is set many years before Harry and his friends go to Hogwarts. And more projects are being planned. Although Rowling's work has made her wealthy, the author has not forgotten her early struggles. The money earned from many of her newest works goes to charitable causes.

J. K. Rowling is one of the most successful writers of our time. But there are many other outstanding women in literature. Some of their names are not as familiar. Some have written pieces that are read all over the world. Others write for smaller audiences. But all have something to say.

Explore Online

Chapter One is about J. K. Rowling. The chapter talks about her success with the Harry Potter series and her later work. Rowling's website has additional information about the author and her writing. Does the website answer any additional questions you had about Rowling? What new information did you learn from the website?

J. K. Rowling
abdocorelibrary.com/women-in-literature

Women Who Wrote Classics

Sometimes stories or poems live on long after their authors are dead. They become classic pieces of literature. They are studied in school. People talk about what the stories mean. Some of these works are adapted into movies. Many works of classic literature were written by women.

JANE AUSTEN

Jane Austen was born in England in the late 1700s. As a young adult, Austen began writing novels. One of them she called *Elinor and Marianne*. The story was told in a series of letters. Later the book became *Sense and*

Jane Austen's books are still popular today.

Pride and Prejudice has been adapted into many different film versions.

Sensibility. Austen had an active social life. She also helped run the family home. But she always found time to write.

Austen began publishing her work under the name "A Lady" when she was in her 30s. She published *Sense and Sensibility*, *Pride and Prejudice*, *Mansfield Park*, and *Emma* between 1811 and 1816. Her books are known for their romantic plots and their focus on manners in society. They remain popular in classrooms and libraries. *Pride and Prejudice* is the most popular. Pride makes Elizabeth Bennet and Fitzwilliam Darcy argue at first, but eventually they fall in love.

CHARLOTTE BRONTË

Charlotte Brontë was born in England during the early 1800s. She came from a family of writers and began writing early. In 1847, she published *Jane Eyre* under the pen name Currer Bell. The book was an immediate hit. The main character, Jane, is an orphan growing up in a harsh school. She later falls in love with her employer and ends up marrying him. Brontë published three other books before her death in 1855.

The Queen of Horror

Mary Shelley began writing as a child. She published her first poem through her father's company at the age of ten. Her most famous story, *Frankenstein*, tells about a man who makes a monster. Shelley wrote the novel in response to a challenge from another famous writer, Lord Byron. Her monster tale was first published in 1818. The book featured an introduction by her husband, Percy Bysshe Shelley. The book was a great success, but the author's name remained a secret for several years.

LOUISA MAY ALCOTT

Louisa May Alcott was born in Germantown, Pennsylvania, in 1832. During her lifetime, she worked hard to become a successful author. This was partly to help support her family. Alcott began publishing poems, short stories, adventure tales, and children's stories as early as 1851. In 1862, she began writing plays that were produced in theaters in Boston, Massachusetts. These stories were published under different pen names.

In approximately 1863, Alcott began writing under her

The Classics in the Movies

Most authors of what we consider to be classics were long dead when movies were invented. Nevertheless, these classic pieces are the subject of many movies. Charlotte Brontë's *Jane Eyre* has been made into many movies. Her sister Emily's *Wuthering Heights* also has several movie versions. Mary Ann Evans, pen name George Eliot, was the author of *Daniel Deronda* and *Middlemarch*. Both books have been brought to life in film. Alcott's *Little Women* has been released as a motion picture several times.

THE PEN NAMES OF
WOMEN

Look at the graphic showing pen names used by female authors. Some authors might use initials instead of their full names. Think about the reasons a writer might want to do this. Why do you think women writing in the 1800s used pen names? Why do you think women might use pen names today? Have the reasons changed?

Book	Pen Name	Birth Name	Year First Released
Valentine	George Sand	Amantine Dupin	1832
Wuthering Heights	Ellis Bell	Emily Brontë	1847
Middlemarch	George Eliot	Mary Ann Evans	1871
Five Children and It	E. Nesbit	Edith Nesbit	1902
Mary Poppins	P. L. Travers	Pamela Lyndon Travers	1934
Harry Potter	J. K. Rowling	Joanne Rowling	1997

Little Women has been adapted into a movie several times. This image is from the 1994 film.

own name. She wrote for the *Atlantic Monthly* and *Lady's Companion*. She also became an editor of a girls' magazine. Her first novel, *Little Women*, was published in 1868. Its success gave her the financial freedom she desired. The stories are based on things that happened to Alcott and her sisters while they were growing up.

STRAIGHT TO THE
SOURCE

In December 1856, Louisa May Alcott made the following entry in her journal. She mentions members of her family, including her sisters May and Betty:

> *Busy with Christmas and New Year's tales. Heard a good lecture by E. P. Whipple on "Courage." Thought I needed it, being rather tired of living like a spider, spinning my brains out for money. . . .*
>
> *Now board [rent] is all safe, and something over for home, if stories and sewing fail. I don't do much, but can send little comforts to Mother and Betty, and keep May neat.*

Source: "Louisa May Alcott, Her Life, Letters, and Journals." *Internet Archive*. Internet Archive, 1889. Web. Accessed November 21, 2017.

Back It Up

Earning a living as a writer became important to Alcott early in her life. She often mentioned earning money in her letters and journals. What evidence do you find in this entry to back this up? Write down two or three points from the entry that lead you to this conclusion.

Women of Poetry

Poetry has been the language of love and emotion for centuries. Sometimes poetry uses rhyme and rhythm to create a musical quality. Sometimes poetry uses other literary devices to cause the reader to think or feel a certain way. Many women have proven themselves masters at creating powerful poetry.

ELIZABETH BARRETT BROWNING

Elizabeth Barrett Browning was born Elizabeth Barrett in England in 1806. Educated at home, Barrett began reading and writing early. By the

Elizabeth Barrett Browning was a famous Victorian poet.

age of 14 she published her first book, titled *The Battle of Marathon*.

Despite challenges with her health and the family's finances, Barrett wrote constantly. Barrett's work became popular with the public and made her an established poet. It also caught the attention of fellow poet Robert Browning. During a two-year period, the pair exchanged nearly 600 letters. In 1846, they married, and Barrett became Elizabeth Barrett Browning. She released a collection of poems in 1850, titled *Sonnets from the Portuguese*. It contained poems written to Robert during their courtship. In 1856, Browning published the epic poem *Aurora Leigh*. The main character, Aurora, is raised by her father in Florence and grows up to be a writer. Scholars praise its early work of promoting equality between genders.

EMILY DICKINSON

Emily Dickinson was an American writer and poet. She was born in Amherst, Massachusetts, in 1830.

As a young girl, Dickinson was sent to school. She was an excellent student. But she was too shy to feel comfortable around unfamiliar people. Dickinson returned home in 1848 and remained in Amherst with her family for the rest of her life.

Dickinson began writing while still a teenager. She wrote hundreds of poems but only published a few while she was alive. Dickinson wrote poems that did not always rhyme or use regular punctuation. Many of her poems use images from nature to describe feelings. In one poem, she compares hope to a bird.

Dickinson's family did not realize how much she had

Poetry Firsts

In 1650, Anne Bradstreet became the first published American poet. In 1773, Phillis Wheatley was the first African American to publish a book of poetry. In 1950, Gwendolyn Brooks became the first African American to win a Pulitzer Prize. Elizabeth Woody, named as Oregon's state poet in 2016, was the first American Indian to be named an official state poet.

written until after her death in 1886. The first book of her poems was published in 1890. Other volumes followed. Dickinson lived on in her work. She quickly became one of America's best-known poets.

Forms of Poetry

Not all poetry is the same. Some poetry is structured. It follows a certain pattern. There are rules for the number of syllables per line and which words must rhyme. Some poetry is less structured. But it still follows a certain pattern. And some poetry has no pattern at all. It flows freely from the mind of the author. Most poetry is written to share emotions. It causes the reader to feel something in response.

MAYA ANGELOU

Maya Angelou was the professional name of Marguerite Annie Johnson Angelopoulos. Her brother called her Maya when they were young. During her lifetime, Angelou was an author, screenwriter, poet, actress, dancer, and civil rights activist. She received many honors and awards. Angelou's first major work was a memoir called *I Know Why the Caged Bird Sings.* It is about her childhood spent at different times with

Maya Angelou recites "On the Pulse of Morning" at President Bill Clinton's inauguration in 1993.

either her mother or grandmother. It became the first nonfiction best seller ever written by a black woman. Although the book is written in prose, it has a poetic quality to it. It reads almost like poetry.

In 1971, Angelou published her best-known collection of poetry. *Just Give Me a Cool Drink of Water 'Fore I Die* was nominated for the Pulitzer Prize. When she died in 2014, many famous people attended her memorial service.

CHAPTER
FOUR

The Storytellers

Telling stories has been a form of entertainment for generations. A good story has the power to transport the reader to faraway places. It can help readers see things in different ways. Stories can cause readers to laugh or cry or think. Some of the best storytellers are women.

AGATHA CHRISTIE

Agatha Christie was an English author and playwright who wrote more than 200 novels, stories, and plays. Her first published work appeared in 1920. *The Mysterious Affair at Styles* introduced the Belgian detective Hercule Poirot. In 1930, Christie created Miss Marple, another crime-solving

Agatha Christie's mysteries are still popular today.

character. Poirot and Marple became two of Christie's best-known characters.

Although Christie died in 1976, her novels are still widely read. Billions of copies have been sold. And dozens of them have been made into movies. One of Christie's most famous titles is *Murder on the Orient Express.* A new movie version of the book was released in 2017.

TONI MORRISON

Toni Morrison is an American author who writes about the black American experience. Her first novel was published in 1970. Although *The Bluest Eye* did not sell well at first, Morrison continued to write. She also worked as a fiction editor for a large US publishing house. Her second novel, *Sula*, tells the story of two black women's friendship from childhood to death. *Sula* was nominated for the American Book Award. Morrison's third novel, *Song of Solomon*, published in 1977, also gained national attention.

In the 1980s, Morrison wrote two more novels. One of them, *Beloved,* is based on the true story of a runaway slave. The novel earned her a Pulitzer Prize for fiction in 1988. In 1993, Morrison became the first African American woman to win a Nobel Prize in Literature. Since then, Morrison has written many more novels. One of her most recent is *God Help the Child*, which was published in 2015. Morrison also received the Presidential Medal of Freedom for her work. The medal is the highest national award that can be given to a civilian.

Sandra Cisneros

Sandra Cisneros grew up in Chicago in the 1950s and 1960s with six brothers. When she was older, she wrote *The House on Mango Street*. Some of the stories in the book were inspired by Cisneros's childhood. The book has become a classic. It has sold more than 6 million copies since it was published in 1984. It highlights Latino culture and helped other Americans appreciate Latino life. Cisneros has also written poetry, a children's book, novels, and short stories.

Octavia Butler

When Octavia Butler was nine years old she saw the science fiction movie *Devil Girl from Mars*. Butler decided she could write a better story and liked the idea of being paid for it. Butler went on to become an award-winning science fiction author. Her work combined fantasy with real-life issues. She was the first science fiction writer to receive a fellowship grant from the MacArthur Foundation. She was also the first black woman to receive Hugo and Nebula Awards, which are some of the top awards for science fiction.

AMY TAN

Amy Tan is a Chinese American author. She wrote the best-selling novel *The Joy Luck Club.* The book is about the relationship between Chinese women and their Chinese American daughters. It was published in 1989. *The Joy Luck Club* was a best seller for several months. It has been translated into 25 languages and made into a movie.

Tan has written several other novels and children's books. Her novels were well received and have also appeared on best-seller lists. Her children's book,

CHARACTER TYPES

 HERO The main character, or protagonist, who wants something in the story.

 VILLAIN The less likable character, or antagonist, who tries to keep the hero from getting what he or she wants.

 **MENTOR** Someone with more knowledge or experience who helps the hero.

 **SIDEKICK** Someone who is less skilled than the hero but helps in other ways.

The women in this chapter are master storytellers. They create characters that keep their readers interested throughout the book. According to the infographic, what are some common types of characters? Think about your favorite book. Can you name the characters from the book that fill these roles?

The Chinese Siamese Cat, was made into a television show for the PBS network.

STEPHENIE MEYER

Stephenie Meyer is the best-selling author of the Twilight book series. The books tell the story of Bella

Stephenie Meyer, *left*, signs a film poster for her Twilight series.

Swan, who falls in love with a vampire. In 2003, Meyer was a busy stay-at-home mom when the idea for *Twilight* came to her in a dream. *Twilight* was released in 2005 and quickly became a best seller. Meyer went on to write three more books in the series. All four have been made into movies. The series sold more than 250 million copies in its first 10 years and has been translated into 37 languages.

STRAIGHT TO THE
SOURCE

In a 2015 interview, Toni Morrison talked about her writing with National Public Radio:

> *Part of it, for me, is the sound. I'm a radio child with the ear up against the gauze, where you hear stories, you know those little stories they used to play on the radio for 15 minutes. . . . It was such a cooperative thing. If they said . . . "It's storming," you had to see it yourself. If they said "red," you had to identify the shade. So the sound of my mother, the sound of the radio and the fact that they forced us, happily, to tell stories— that was the entertainment in the pre-television days. . . . For me, the sound of the text is very important—so important that I read all of my books for the audiobooks so that the reader can hear what I hear.*

> Source: Terry Gross. "Interview: Toni Morrison, Author of 'God Help the Child.'" *NPR*. NPR, April 20, 2015. Web. Accessed November 21, 2017.

What's the Big Idea?
Read the passage carefully. What does Morrison say is the most important part of her writing? How did it become so important? What does she do that helps her readers relate to this element in her writing?

CHAPTER FIVE

Children's Authors

Adults who write children's books at any level tell stories that appeal to kids. Readers fondly remember these books into adulthood. Many of the best children's writers are women.

BEVERLY CLEARY

Beverly Cleary had trouble reading when she was a kid. It gave her a special understanding of the challenges some children have with reading. It made her want to write stories even struggling readers could enjoy. Her first book was published in 1950. *Henry Huggins*

Kate DiCamillo is among today's most popular children's authors.

is a story about a regular boy who befriends a dog named Ribsy.

Following the success of Henry, Cleary wrote stories about other regular kids. She wrote a series of books about Henry's friend Beezus and her little sister Ramona. The books explore Ramona's life from preschool through fourth grade. She goes to school, fights with her sister, and plays with the neighbors.

Cleary's books have been sold in more than 20 countries and 14 languages. Cleary was awarded the Newberry Medal for the best children's

Beverly Cleary's books have many fans.

book for *Dear Mr. Henshaw* in 1984. Cleary has won many other awards as well. In 2000, the Library of Congress gave her its Living Legend award for all of her work.

JUDY BLUME

Judy Blume began her writing career in the 1960s. She was a young mother looking for a way to express all the stories inside her head. Her first book was published

Judy Blume's books have sold more than 85 million copies.

in 1969. In 1970, she wrote her first novel. *Iggie's House* is about a black family that moves into a white neighborhood. Later that year she wrote *Are You There God? It's Me, Margaret.* This book is about a young girl growing up.

By the mid-1970s, Blume was firmly established as a writer of novels for teens. Many of them are about sensitive topics such as bullying, puberty, and divorce. Titles such as *Tales of a Fourth*

Grade Nothing, Blubber, and *Superfudge* became best sellers. Blume has sold more than 85 million books. Her work has been translated into 32 languages.

CARMEN AGRA DEEDY

Carmen Agra Deedy was born in Cuba, but she came to America as a refugee when she was young. Her first book was a collection of stories about when she was growing up. Some of her other books also depict Latino culture. *Martina the Beautiful Cockroach* is about a cockroach deciding who to marry. Martina's grandma has surprising advice for her. The book is based on a Cuban folktale.

Deedy has written several picture books for kids. Some of them are funny. *The Library Dragon* tells about a dragon who tries to be a school librarian. She has also written picture books about real-life events. *The Yellow Star* tells how the people of Denmark protected Jews during World War II (1939–1945).

KATE DICAMILLO

Kate DiCamillo was sick a lot as a child. The time she spent alone in bed imagining and observing things helped shape her as a writer. DiCamillo earned a degree in English in 1987. A few years later, she took a job in a book warehouse. The warehouse gave her the opportunity to read children's fiction. She soon fell in love with it.

DiCamillo's first novel was published in 2000. *Because of Winn-Dixie* is a story about a little girl dealing with the loss of her mother. The book was released as a movie in 2005. Other books by DiCamillo include *The Tale of Despereaux*, published in 2003. Despereaux is a mouse who falls in love with a

Beatrix Potter

Beatrix Potter was a British writer and illustrator born in 1866. She wrote and illustrated more than 20 children's books. Peter Rabbit, Jemima Puddle-Duck, and Benjamin Bunny are among her most memorable characters. Potter went on to write more animal stories that have become children's classics.

princess. A movie version was released in 2008. In 2014, DiCamillo was awarded the Newberry Medal for another novel. *Flora & Ulysses: The Illuminated Adventures* is about a comic-book-loving girl and a squirrel. DiCamillo has also written an early chapter book series and some picture books.

Women have been writing stories for a very long time. Today, many women write different types of stories for different people. No matter what type of story people like best, they can find something they will love to read because of these authors.

Further Evidence

One of the authors discussed in Chapter Five is Beverly Cleary. What was the main point of this section? Find two or three pieces of evidence that support this point. Then visit the website below. What information does it have that wasn't in this book?

Beverly Cleary
abdocorelibrary.com/women-in-literature

NOTABLE
WORKS

Little Women by Louisa May Alcott

Louisa May Alcott's *Little Women* is a classic novel about
a family of four girls. It is loosely based on Alcott's own
family. The story takes place during and after the Civil
War (1861–1865). In the book, three of the sisters become
adults, marry, and have children. Many of the events of *Little
Women* were part of Alcott's experiences.

The Joy Luck Club by Amy Tan

Amy Tan's book *The Joy Luck Club* explores the relationship
between traditional Chinese mothers and their Chinese
American daughters. Three mothers and four daughters
share their stories in separate sections of the book. Each
part begins with a parable related to the Chinese game they
play. Tan has won numerous awards for the book. She also
cowrote the screenplay for the movie.

Dear Mr. Henshaw by Beverly Cleary

Dear Mr. Henshaw is a middle-grade novel about divorce.
Beverly Cleary wrote the book at the request of one of

her readers. In it, a boy deals with his parents' divorce by writing letters to his favorite author. He only sends some of the letters, but writing each one helps him deal with the changes in his life. The book received a Newberry Medal in 1984.

STOP AND
THINK

Dig Deeper

After reading this book, what questions do you still have about any of the authors mentioned? With an adult's help, find a few reliable resources that can help you answer your questions. Write a paragraph about what you learned.

Take a Stand

In Chapter Five you learned that Judy Blume usually writes books about topics that are sensitive. Through the years, Blume has written books about topics such as racism, puberty, religion, body image, divorce, and teen sex. Do you think it is a good idea for her to cover these types of topics in her books? Why or why not?

You Are There

Imagine you are able to meet one of the authors in this book. Write a letter telling your friends what the author is like and what you talked about. What did you learn about this author? Be sure to add plenty of detail.

Say What?

Much of this book is about writing, publishing, and women who write. Because you may not be familiar with writing as a career, some of the vocabulary may be new to you. Find five words in this book you've never heard before. Use a dictionary to find out what they mean. Then write the meanings in your own words, and use each word in a new sentence.

GLOSSARY

adapt
taking a book and making it into a movie or TV show

civilian
someone who is not a member of the military

courtship
the period of getting to know one another in a romantic relationship

memoir
a record or account of a person's own life experiences

pen name
a name used in place of an author's real name

prequel
a book, play, or movie that takes place before a related story

refugee
someone who has to leave his or her country because it's not safe there

rejected
refused or turned down

screenplay
the written form of a story that is made into a movie

sensitive
something that is usually not discussed in public

ONLINE
RESOURCES

To learn more about women in literature, visit our free resource websites below.

Visit **abdocorelibrary.com** for free Common Core resources for teachers and students, including vetted activities, multimedia, and booklinks, for deeper subject comprehension.

Visit **abdobooklinks.com** for free additional online weblinks for further learning. These links are routinely monitored and updated to provide the most current information available.

LEARN
MORE

Angelou, Maya. *Poetry for Young People: Maya Angelou*. New York: Sterling Publishing, 2013.

Fromowitz, Lori. *Louisa May Alcott*. Minneapolis, MN: Abdo Publishing, 2013

INDEX

About the Author

Wendy Hinote Lanier is a native Texan and former elementary teacher who writes and speaks for children and adults on a variety of topics. She is the author of more than 25 books for children and young people.

48